Weavers of the World

Contents

A World of Weaving

People all over the world weave.
They weave to make useful things, and
they weave to make
beautiful things.
Often the things they make are
both beautiful and useful.

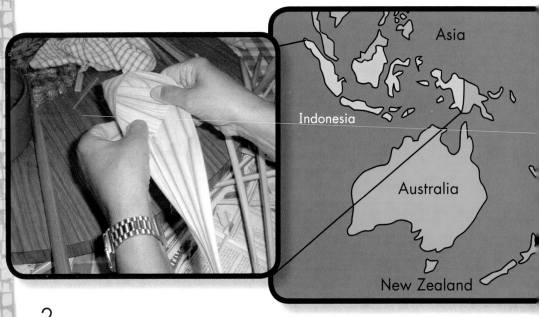

Asia

Indonesia

Australia

New Zealand

North
America

Appalachian
region

Africa

Ghana

Peru

South
America

3

Appalachia

A mountain woman makes blankets
for her family.
She spins her own yarn.
She colors the yarn with plants
that grow near her home.

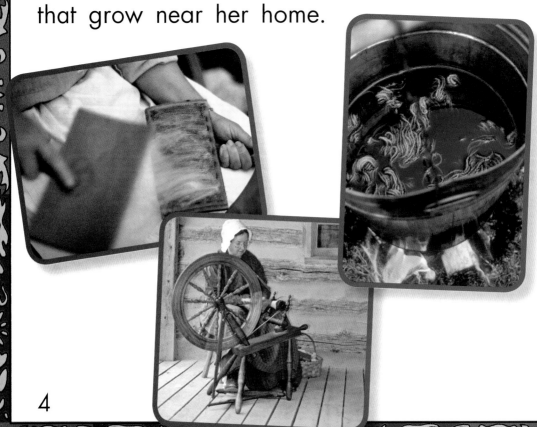

Then she weaves the blankets.

This is a blanket called a coverlet,
woven in the mountains of Appalachia.

These blankets are beautiful,
but also useful.
High up in the mountains,
it is very cold at night!

Ghana

This man weaves strips of bright cloth. Long ago, he learned how to weave from his father.

Now, he shows his son how to weave.

Each pattern on this cloth
has a special meaning.
The butterfly means hard work.
The pineapple means friendship.

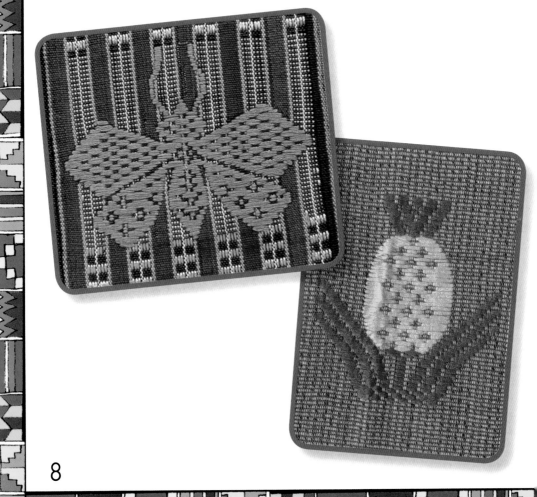

Long ago, this cloth was made just for important people. Now anyone can wear it for special times.

This is kente cloth from Ghana. The word *kente* comes from a word that means "basket" because the cloth looks woven like a basket.

Peru

In this mountain village, children learn to weave when they are six or seven.

They learn by watching
grown-ups weave.

People in Peru weave their blankets
with yarn made from the wool
of their sheep and llamas.

Indonesia

Indonesia has many different islands. Each island has its own kind of weaving.

Some weavers use leaves to make bags and hats. Weaving can even be used to make things for cooking. Rice cakes are wrapped up in woven leaves.

The ketupat is a rice cake wrapped in woven coconut leaves.

Other weavers cut stems from palm trees and weave them into baskets.

Weavers from around the world bring us many beautiful and useful things.

Index